GOSSAMER BOOKS

Abraham Lincoln
The Civil War President

Art: Saral Tiwari
Script: Ginger Turner

ISBN: 0-9742-5020-1

Suggested Cataloging
Turner, Ginger.
    Abraham Lincoln: The Civil War President/ by Saral Tiwari, Ginger Turner
        p. cm. – (Famous Americans)
    Summary: Portrays Lincoln's life as a father, statesman, and president during the Civil War years.
    ISBN: 0-9742-5020-1
    1. Lincoln, Abraham, 1809-1865 – Juvenile literature.
    2. Presidents – United States – Biography – Juvenile literature [1. Lincoln, Abraham, 1809-1865. 2. Presidents.]
    I. Title. II. Series

ATTENTION: SCHOOLS AND LIBRARIES
Quality discounts are available with quantity purchases for educational use.
For information, email info@gossamerbooks.com

www.gossamerbooks.com

Abraham Lincoln

The year is 1861. The United States of America is on the brink of war.

Slavery is a way of life across the South. On large plantations and small farms alike, farmers buy and sell black people like cattle.

Meanwhile, in the North, people are starting to regard slavery as a moral evil that must be extinguished before it invades the rest of the country.

Pioneers are opening up vast new territories in the West and, one by one, the territories are becoming states. On the frontier, settlers from the North and South fight for control of the new territory.

Both North and South want to decide the slavery question, but the new states want to decide for themselves.

The West becomes a battleground for burnings, lynching, and assassinations.

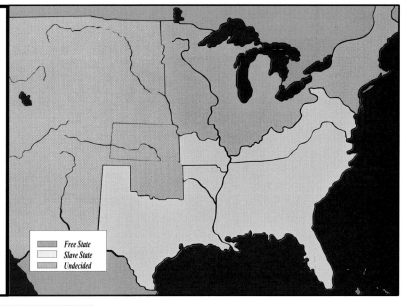

Free State
Slave State
Undecided

Even on the floor of Congress, violence has broken out, as politicians furiously debate slavery. While Senator Charles Sumner is speaking, Congressman Preston Brooks leaps to the floor ...

.... and beats him almost to death with a cane.

Southern slave states decide to leave the country and form a new one, elect their own president, and defend their way of life . . .

....by force if necessary.

One man is chosen to try keep the country's differences from tearing it in two, but only if he can survive the challenge ...

Springfield, Illinois. Feb 11, 1861.

Are you leaving already?

Almost, Mr. Roll. Just a few last things to settle.

I'll miss hearing your stories, Mr. Lincoln. They always did brighten my day, but don't worry. I'll take good care of Old Bob.

It's a shame to say goodbye to Old Bob. But I don't suppose he'd fit into the White House. He'd miss the fields of Illinois.

Will you be taking the little dog along, Mr. Lincoln?

Oh, please, pa, can't we take him along? He'll be awfully good. I'll take care of him.

Old Fido would not survive the long train ride from Illinois to Washington. Maybe it's better that he stays here and lives with Mr. Roll's boys.

Later that day . . .

Excuse me, sir. I am looking for Mr. Lincoln.

He is giving his farewell speech to the town of Springfield. Let's go hear him speak.

My friends, no one, not in my situation, can appreciate my

... feeling of sadness at this parting. To this place, and the kindness of these people, I owe everything. Here I have lived a quarter of a century, and have passed from a young to an old man. Here my children have been born, and one is buried.

I've just come straight from Chicago with an urgent message from Allan Pinkerton.

Allan Pinkerton! The famous private detective!!?! What could he want with Ol' Abe?

Mr. Lincoln!

Springfield train station.

I'm afraid I must say goodbye. Take care, mother.

You're the smartest man I know, Abraham. You taught yourself everything, without even going to school.

4

You always encouraged me to keep learning, Ma ...

You're a good man, but the country is tearing itself apart, and you will get caught in the middle! No man, not even you, can fix it.

I am afraid that something will happen to you, and I will never see you again.

No, no, Mama. All will be well.

I will be back here some day. I promise.

Mr. Lincoln! Is he here?

Is that his train just gone, ma'am?

My boy has just left for Washington to become President.

Oh, no! He may never get there if I don't reach him first!

Have you seen a little dog? He answers to the name of Fido.

The next day at Ferrandini's barber shop in Baltimore, Maryland.

You're keeping it short. A clean military hairstyle. Are you planning to join the troops soon?

Why? Do you think there will be war?

Ha, ha, ha! Of course. We are practically at war already. The whole city of Baltimore is buzzing with rumors. When Lincoln comes here, he had better watch his neck!

Hmm. And you? Will you join the rebel army?

Philadelphia train station

DELPHIA

All aboard! Is everything ready?

Almost, sir. There's a very sick man who must get to his doctor straight away. He's being brought on board right now.

Hey, there, ol' boy. Are you looking for your owner?

You'd better tell that dog to scram. We can't have any stray animals aboard.

Hear that, friend? Time to go. No dogs are allowed here.

Well, don't talk to him, or he'll follow you around wanting food . . .

Last call for Baltimore!

Excuse me. Is this President-elect Lincoln's train?

No, sir. Mr. Lincoln changed his travel schedule. He's not going to Washington today after all.

Inside the train . . .

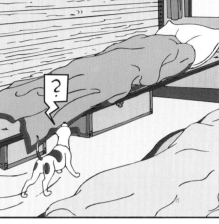

This here's Baltimore! Any passengers going on to Washington D.C. must be back on the train in one hour.

SLAVE AUCTION

Sale!
?

I've got a good-looking girl slave here. Fifteen years old. Worth at least $1000! I've got $1000 from the man in the green jacket. Who can beat that?

Hmm, I've seen this before . .

We're not in Illinois any more, Fido...

New Orleans famous French quarters...

Slave auction!

I have a strong slave here ...

Louisiana is a slave state. Human beings, boys and girls, sold like lumber. Those people are treated worse than dogs. If ever I get a chance to hit slavery, I will hit it hard!

Sold for $1300! I've got another slave here. He's the girl's brother, ten years old His name is Eli.

Ah, Eli! I'll come back for you!

Shh! Not a word, or someone may recognize you.

I must find out who buys him.

I've got $600 from the man in the red hat!

All aboard for Washington D.C.!

We don't have time. Come, let's get out of here!

The next morning, Feb. 23, 1861. Abe finally arrives in Washington, D.C.

WASHINGT

WASHINGTON RAILWAY STATION

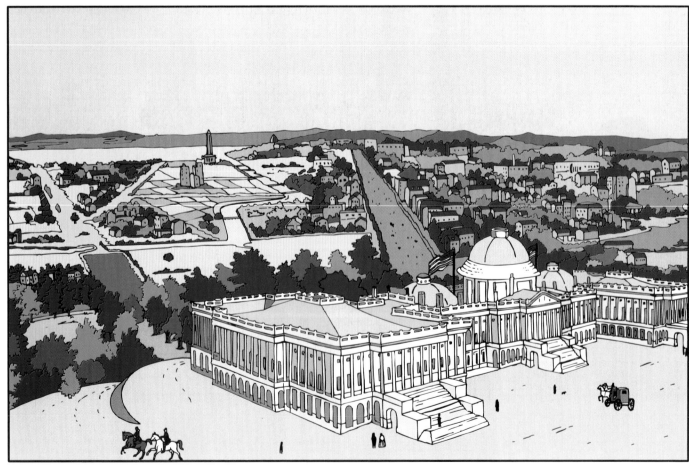

Welcome to Washington, Mr. Lincoln, and congratulations on the successful trip!

Papa!

Where's Fido? I've lost the poor dog again!

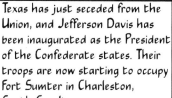
Texas has just seceded from the Union, and Jefferson Davis has been inaugurated as the President of the Confederate states. Their troops are now starting to occupy Fort Sumter in Charleston, South Carolina.

Do you think we will go to war, Mr. President?

The Union will survive, or take me down with it.

Meanwhile...

Samson, I've got to send a letter in the post office. Colored people aren't allowed inside. Wait right here...

Hey, there, little dog.

The White House. April 14, 1861. The war is now fully underway...

The President will be with you in a moment, Mr. Douglas.

Yeeeeeeee-haaaaa-haaaa!

Oh, hello! What do we have here?

Sorry, sir. I was just crossing the Mississippi with my oxen. We're on the way west to the wild frontier. Are you new around these parts?

Um, yes.

Wanna come on a Gold Rush? I have room in the wagon. We'll go to California and get rich!

Actually, I'm just waiting to see the President...

Oh, are you a friend of pa's?

I expect it will be a long and hard one—but of course, nothing can be harder than twelve hours a day of chopping wood in Illinois!

On you rests the future of our United States. It's time for us old enemies to make friends. I wish you the best of luck in this war.

Thank you. I only hope that someday, the North and South can follow your example.

Now, let's all go for dinner and swap stories!

As the Union army continually changes its Generals, Confederates under the leadership of General "Stonewall" Jackson and Commander General Robert E. Lee surprise the Union forces in the battles of Bull Run and The Seven Day Battle...

... yet suffer heavy casualties of their own.

March 8, 1862: Confederates make naval history when they use an iron ship Merrimac to ram into the wooden Union ships to break the blockade. . .

The next day, U.S.S. Monitor arrives in time to challenge Merrimac. A new age of naval warfare has dawned. The submarine has been used for the first time . . .

At Shiloh, the Confederate troops fight bravely and surprise the Union forces with their superior tactics. The Union army eventually wins this battle. However, the generals now know that the war will not be short ...

... and would be one "bloody affair!"

I didn't actually do it. But Charles Allen hated me and lied.

It was just my word against his, and I couldn't think of a way in the world that I could escape. I needed the best lawyer. I went to Abe...

I didn't do it, Mr. Lincoln

But the story gets more complicated...

You can't help Jack Armstrong's son! Don't you remember how this boy's father treated you when you first came to town?

I will not judge a man because of his father's past mistakes.

What? As your law partner and friend, I must protest!

You know you can't stop me once I've set my mind to something, Mr. Herndon.

Charles Allen claimed to be the only witness. Abe questioned him over and over in court, trying to find a hole in his story...

Did you actually see the fight?

Yes!

And you stood near to them?

No, it was one hundred fifty feet or more.

In the open field?

No, in the timber.

What kind of timber?

Beech timber.

Leaves rather thick on it in August?
It looks like it.

What time did all this take place?
Eleven o'clock at night

Did you have a candle there?
No, what would I want a candle for?

How could you see from one-hundred fifty feet, without a candle, at eleven o'clock at night?
The moon was shining real bright.

Full moon?
Yes, a full moon!

Ah ha! But look here. Doesn't it say that on August 29th, the moon was barely past the first quarter?

There is no way you could have seen Mr. Armstrong commit the crime!

I owe him my life.
So Abe saved you with the light of the moon!

Hey, Duff. Got a letter for you here. Real nice handwriting on it too.
Who's it from?

It's from Mary.

Mary? Ooh!

It's a miracle! You've brought me the best news a father could ever dream of.

You sure do look like Abe's little dog. That man showed me a great forgiveness. I never treated him right when he first came to Springfield ...

I challenged him to a wrestling match in front of the whole town to try to embarrass him. He put all that behind him when my son needed help... I just hope he will remember that forgiveness for each captured Confederate soldier!

As the war wages on, Lee invades the North. In turn, Lincoln sends General McClellan to pursue the Confederate invaders and deal a decisive blow...

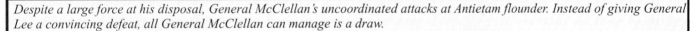

Despite a large force at his disposal, General McClellan's uncoordinated attacks at Antietam flounder. Instead of giving General Lee a convincing defeat, all General McClellan can manage is a draw.

The battle of Antietam proved to be the deadliest single day of the war...

... with thousands of Union and Confederate losses.

Two months later: Nov. 7, 1862. Lincoln's office in the White House

I simply don't understand why you continue to interfere, Mr. Lincoln. I've told you that I am handling the situation.

Certainly, General McClellan. But I would prefer that you handle it a little faster.

The army is getting cold, General!

The troops are training, organizing. They have to recover after the fighting in Maryland.

It has been two months since the victory at Antietam, and we have made no progress since then. I gave you command of the entire Union army last year, and we have suffered losses left and right.

We won at Antietam, but 23,000 men had to die. For what? So you can sit around and wait for another rebel attack? No, General!

You can't expect me to do everything at once!

If you don't want to use the army, I'd like to borrow it for a while. I'm removing you from your post, General McClellan.

Hmph! I should like to see you try to command it yourself.

I agree, Mr. President. You should remove him from his position. Find another general. But who?

I shall let you return to work. We have dragged our feet for too long, gentlemen. Soldiers are on the fields as we speak in the freezing cold, awaiting direction from their leaders. Let's not disappoint them!

If you really want to save the Union, Mr. President, you will act now to wipe out slavery.

Look, Pa! See the handsome uniform Mr. Stanton gave me. He said I'm a real general now. I even have troops. Stand at attention, men!

What's happening, Pa? Are you all right?

Yes, Tad. When I think of the sacrifice yet to be offered, my heart feels like lead inside me. This war is the hardest thing I've ever taken on. Sometimes I don't believe we will win.

Why?

I've just fired General McClellan. No one else can help me. I must command the troops by myself.

You're not on your own, pa. I'm a soldier now. I will help you.

Thank you, General Tad!

Mr. President, sorry to interrupt...

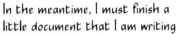

Six months later June 30, 1863. Gettysburg.

Mail's here! Get your mail!

Howdy, what's this? They're sending slaves to deliver the mail now, are they?

I am not a slave, sir. I've been freed by the Emancipation Proclamation. Don't you know you're in the free state of Pennsylvania now?

Beg pardon, I just never seen a colored mailman, that's all. Thank you. Hey, another letter for Duff.

Are you going into the fighting soon?

Don't ask me. I just shoot when they tell me to. But I reckon we'll see some action here!

Gee, I'd like to get in on that.

First, you become a mailman, and now you want to be a soldier! You've got some guts. We sure could use you!

Yes, sir. Well, good luck to you. Good day.

Hmm, this bag got a lot heavier.

Hey, I know you! Coming back with me to the city, are you?

A month later, August 8, 1863. Another Cabinet meeting in the White House...

After two years of war, we have finally gained a decisive victory at Gettysburg.

But we cannot be sure of victory, yet...

Waaaaaaaahhh!!!

Huh?

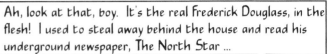

Hmm... you smell like my boy, Tad ... wonder where you came from.

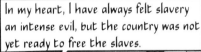

Teach the rebels that the price they are to pay must be the abolition of slavery!

The next day. Lincoln's office, The White House.

It is a pleasure to see you, Mr. Douglass. You have been one of my greatest critics...

You may remember that you were not always against slavery!

In my heart, I have always felt slavery an intense evil, but the country was not yet ready to free the slaves.

Still, you started fighting the war to keep national power over the southern states only...

But we can end it with freeing the slaves. Ah, I may be a slow mover, but I never move backward. We will get to freedom eventually!

Your Emancipation Proclamation was well spoken, Mr. President, but ...

But still not enough?

You know it will not hold forever. Any President after you can change it...

...at the drop of a hat, Mr. Lincoln. We need a freedom that can never be taken away. You must win this war and make sure that slavery is gone forever!

You are right, my friend. The Proclamation is only a wartime measure. Much of the South will not even obey it. To free the slaves, we would need to change the country's constitution!

But first, you need a country. To save the country, you must defeat the rebels. Let the slaves enlist in the army and help to fight for their own freedom!

Blacks in the army?

Two months later. Nov. 19, 1863, Gettysburg battlefield.

Here we are, boy. The sight of that terrible battle. Now it has gone down in history.

Look boy, here he comes now. The President himself to make his speech. What a tall man!

Can you believe what a giant battle took place here not long ago?

Four score and seven years ago our fathers brought forth upon this continent a new nation, conceived in liberty, and dedicated to...

... the proposition that all men are created equal.

Now we are engaged in a great civil war, testing whether that nation, or any nation so conceived, and so dedicated, can long endure. We are met on a great battlefield of war.

Ready... aim... Fire!

We have come to dedicate a portion of that field, as a final resting place for them who have given their lives, that that nation might live. It is altogether fitting and proper that we should do this.

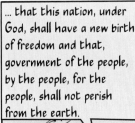

One year later, Sep. 2, 1864.

My second presidential election is coming up.

Who would have guessed that I would be running against my old General McClellan for President?

I'm afraid I will never be reelected now. General Grant tries again and again to attack Richmond. While it stands, my Presidency falls.

I would worry more about your assassination threats than about McClellan.

But McClellan will not keep the slaves free. If he becomes President, everything I have worked for will be lost!

I will die someday, but not until the Union is secure.

I have an urgent message, Mr. President! Down in Georgia, General Sherman has laid siege to Atlanta and left the city in flames. Atlanta is ours! Richmond is next!

Seven months later. April 4, 1865. Richmond, Virginia, the capital of the Confederacy. Abe has been re-elected to his second term ...

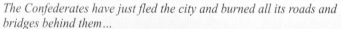

Lee and his rebel army have finally fallen to Grant's invasion.

Congratulations, Mr. President! The war is won!

CLOTHING

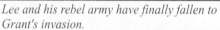

The Confederates have just fled the city and burned all its roads and bridges behind them...

Look, Tad. There it is. The old mansion of Jefferson Davis, President of the Confederacy. Let's have a look inside.

This must be where Davis himself sat, plotting the rebellion that started this terrible war.

So the war is finally won after four long years and 600,000 dead.

The slaves will soon be free. I should be happy now yet I am troubled by strange dreams.

I dreamt I was wandering through the halls ...

Oh, no!

Who is dead?

The President! He was killed by an assassin!

Then came a loud burst which awoke me. Strange that so many have died in this war, and I am still left alive.

Pa?

What's wrong, Tad?

I thought this was the rebel headquarters. Where are all the soldiers?

Some of them ran away with Jefferson Davis.

And what happened to the rest?

Well, the others mostly died in the fighting.

Will I have to die if I am a soldier?

War is a dreadful thing. Of course, everyone has to die eventually, Tad. Even you and me.

Now, let's find you a rebel uniform to show Mr. Stanton and Mama. How does that sound?

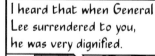

The rebels are in shambles. Our next challenge is reconstructing the South, Mr. President.

Reconstruct? No! Let's teach them a lesson!

I want no more bloodshed. We have already seen enough of that in this war.

Now that the country is finally whole again...

Who are those men?

They were asking to see you, Mr. President, but don't worry. The guards will send them away.

Nonsense! You know that I am always seeing members of the public who come to me. Why would you send them away?

But they are rebels!

The war is over, Stanton. We are all citizens of the United States now.

You must have some regard for your own safety, Mr. President.

Somebody's always plotting an assassination for me. If they had wanted to kill me, they would have done it already. Let's get over that business and send them up.

Five minutes later ...

Mr. President, these men wish to ask for your pardon. This one is a rebel spy caught outside Richmond. And this one is a Union deserter. They are both sentenced to death!

These soldiers have committed serious crimes against the Union! If you let them go, you will undermine your own authority as President.

Well don't you think these boys can do more good above ground than underground?

35

I think it is more important to set an example of forgiveness. I know what it is to lose a son, Mr. Stanton

I want no more boys to die before their time. Pardon them and let them go back to their families.

Now, if you'll excuse me, I have a date with my wife.

That evening ...

FIDO!? Why, I can't believe my eyes!

Ruff!

Is it really you, old boy?

Amazing! I thought I'd lost you years ago on the train. Oh, Fido, what a perfect end to the best of days. Man's best friend has come home at last.

Run to Tad and tell him you are home. I must be off to the theater!

I've never been so happy in my life!

Next day: On the street in Philadelphia

I don't believe it!

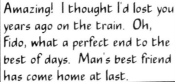

How could they?

In Washington D.C.

36

Folks, I have some terrible news!

Our Abe has just been shot...

They say he was attending a play at Ford's Theater. His bodyguard had slipped ...

... away from his post to get a drink from downstairs.

During the third act, an actor and Confederate supporter named John Wilkes Booth, entered the President's box ...

... and shot him from behind!

He broke his leg in the jump, ...

... yet he managed to escape on a waiting horse in the alley ...

Sic temper tyrannis!

37

... and rode across the border to a Virginia farm, where he was later cornered by the Federal troops and shot!

Five of the best doctors were summoned to help ...

... the President, and they worked all night. The President held onto life, still breathing faintly, but in the end, they could do nothing. Lincoln died at 7:22am this morning.

It says, after his funeral in the White House, his body will be carried to the Capitol dome ...

Thousands of people stand in line, in the rain for hours ...

... just to pass by his coffin.

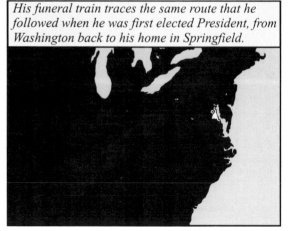

His funeral train traces the same route that he followed when he was first elected President, from Washington back to his home in Springfield.

As the train takes Abe from Chicago to Springfield, ...

... on his final journey ...

.. people wait along the tracks to get a final glimpse of him.

The following day, back in Springfield at last...

No other like him will ever walk the earth. Even those who fought against him must admire him now!

Oh, thank goodness you're alive, Duff!

Huh?

Oh! Excuse me, sir. From a distance, I thought you were someone else.

Did you say Duff?

He's a dear friend of mine from the Union army. I haven't seen him since the battle at Gettysburg.

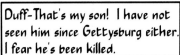
Duff-That's my son! I have not seen him since Gettysburg either. I fear he's been killed.

No! Poor Duff! It can't be true!

We were just a few feet away from each other on the battlefield. I heard a shot whiz past my ear, and I saw him knocked away, ...

... but the smoke was too thick and I could not reach him.

After all that time, I never got a chance to tell him-

By God! I swear I must be going loony. Or else it's the heat...

If my eyes ain't playing tricks on me-HA, HA!

I got a bad case of hallucinations, for I think that's my son in the flesh right now!
?

Pa!
!

My own boy alive again!

I'd just about taken you for dead!

But what happened to you? I thought I saw you fall at Gettysburg.

Right as I saw you, Pa, I got hit. I blacked out for the longest while-and then when I woke in the battlefield hospital, I couldn't remember anything. Only after a few weeks did I discover how I had been wounded ...

.. this one bullet that would have killed me got stuck. I only wish Mary were here!

Looks like you need a new locket, Duff!

But how did you get this? I gave it to-

MARY?! What-how did you-? So it was you fighting alongside me the whole time!

... so here ends our story of Abraham Lincoln, the Civil War President. But his legacy lives on ...

Fact or Fiction

Was Fido's adventure real?

Fido didn't really travel all the way from Illinois to Washington by himself - we made that part up. But Abe did have a little dog named Fido that followed him around. By the time Abe was elected President, Fido was too old to travel and had to be left home at Springfield with Abe's friend John Roll. Fido survived the Civil War and died shortly after Lincoln's assassination.

Did women really fight in the war?

Men were not the only soldiers. Several hundred women fought with them in disguise, bearing arms, charging into battle, and even being wounded, imprisoned, or killed. One woman named Mrs. S.M. Blaylock joined the 26th North Carolina infantry to be close to her husband under the pretended name of John Williams. Sometimes, the women were discovered by accident or if they were wounded, but others disguised themselves as men so well that many of their fellow soldiers never realized who they were!

Were slaves sold in markets?

A slave could be sold for as high as $1,300 in 1861. That's worth about $26,300 today. What Lincoln saw in New Orleans was only a small part of the terrible treatment that black slaves endured before the Civil War.

During the 1800s, over 100,000 slaves escaped through the Underground Railroad. Slaves used this nickname for the secret route they followed to flee to free territories like Canada, Mexico, and the northern United States. Along the route, former slaves and abolitionist sympathizers acted as guides and hosts to help slaves on their dangerous journey.

Want to know more?

Still not sure how much you read here was real? Be your own historian! For more facts about Abe, the Underground Railroad, or the Civil War, look on the Internet, visit www.gossamerbooks.com or go to the local library. There is lots more out there waiting to be uncovered!

Errata

Please refer to the corrected maps below for Pages 12 and 38.

1: Route of President Lincoln's journey for the inauguration (Page 12)

2: Route of President Lincoln's funeral train (Page 38)